How to be Likeable: The Ultimate Guide to Connecting, Relating, and Creating Authentic Lasting Relationship with People

By: Clayton Geoffreys

Table of Contents

Forward

It's not easy being outgoing and social if you're naturally a little bit shy. Social anxiety can often get the best of us when we're faced with new environments and situations that we are not familiar with. However, social interaction is incredibly important and plays a huge role in the opportunities and relationships we are able to cultivate in our lives. Being likeable is important; the way you are perceived by others can often mean the difference between getting that job and not getting that job, or catching that person's interest versus having that person be another person who just walks by. I am not saying you should change you are; but what I am saying is you should challenge yourself to be self-aware and conscious of the importance of social interaction for your psychological and emotional health. Hopefully from reading *How to be Likeable: The Ultimate Guide to Connecting, Relating, and Creating Authentic*

Lasting Relationships with People, I can pass along some of the abundance of information I have learned about why conquering social anxiety is so important and how you can completely change your life by learning how to connect with others. Thank you for purchasing my book. Hope you enjoy and if you do, please do not forget to leave a review! Also, check out my website at claytongeoffreys.com to join my exclusive list where I let you know about my latest books and give you goodies!

Cheers,

Clayton Geoffreys

Why is Social Interaction Important?

'Social' is the singular buzzword that both describes and dictates 21st century living. Almost everyone perceives themselves to be social. Most people have been to a 'social' event, be it an Ice Cream Night at the elementary school or a local singles dance. The concept is not new, and the word itself traces its first use back to the 15th century.[1] However, why is 'social' suddenly so ubiquitous?

'Social' evokes images of carefree social butterflies and refined social graces. It denotes a cheerful disposition and good times. Nothing bad can be said about being social. It is no wonder that the ad world and Internet attach the term to virtually everything. However, 'social' carries more import than dubious buzzwords like 'disambiguate' or 'dog-fooding.' The latter terms are meant to inflate the importance of that to which they refer. 'Disambiguate' simply means clarify, and 'dog-fooding' entails that a company trusts their own products enough to use them. Hence, the terms are little more than business-speak for relatively simplistic ideas. 'Social' is not a simplistic idea. 'Social' is more than IM chats or a busy array of Facebook, Twitter and Reddit icons smattered across a web page. To be social is the fundamental experience of humanity. Humans are animals, and as such, they evolved to be social.[2] It is in our DNA.

It goes without saying that human culture could not have evolved to its present form without a social component. Early man evolved under unimaginably challenging conditions. Our predecessors were confronted with environmental pressures that would be insurmountable without the co-evolution of social interaction. Threats to life arising from predators, exposure to elements and variable availability of food required teamwork to circumvent. This gave rise to social strategies. Social strategies comprise interactions that promoted group survival.[3] While these interactions incurred risk to individuals, the sacrifice one would take was seen as beneficial to all. Collaborative hunting endeavors leading to the death of the aforementioned predators or the acquisition of large game animals—for communal food sharing--are apt examples of the benefits of early social interaction.

Modern man is no longer preoccupied with hunting mammoths and fending off saber-tooth cats. However, the modern man should surely tip his hat to predecessors who evolved the social instincts to tackle these undertakings. Their DNA lives on in our blood, and it provides the foundation from which we humans were able to evolve more complex social structures. Everything from religion to commercial trade to the development of infrastructure required social interaction. It is that important.

The value of social interaction extends beyond large, group enterprises. Individuals need social interaction to thrive in their own personal lives.[4] It is through interaction with others that one learns that his or her life experiences mirror those of others. This promotes a sense of belonging and community. Interaction with others further provides opportunity for recognition of one's achievements, acknowledgement of one's worth and potential endorsements of one's chosen actions. When plagued with self-doubt, fear or sadness, one is particularly vulnerable to this need, for it is only the presence of solicitous others that can alleviate these feelings.

7 Reasons Why Social Interaction is the Secret to Happiness

Social media naysayers would have one believe that social sites like Facebook or MySpace are putting society square on the road to perdition. While cyber-bullying, identity theft and loss of productivity are real problems, the explosion of new forms of social interaction do not necessarily spell the end of civilization. Instead, the many interactions that come from oversharing and dissemination of cat pictures—combined with real life interaction—may actually be driving individual happiness. Why? As shown below, pro-social interaction leads to the acquisition of personal attributes, skills and experiences that are commonly associated with individual happiness.

1. Social   Interaction   Increases   Overall Satisfaction

Social Interaction Increases Overall Social interaction colors how individuals feel about themselves.[5] Numerous, positive interactions with others—online or otherwise—increases personal satisfaction and makes one feel grounded. This is true of both random interactions with coworkers, acquaintances, persons in the public at large, and deep interaction with close friends and family. Whereas the former interactions provide one with a lived sense of community, the latter promotes direct satisfaction. This has been proven repeatedly by many studies.

2. Social Interaction Promotes Learning

Learning cannot occur when one chooses to exist as a proverbial 'island.' Instead, learning mandates exposure to others with new, alternative or opposing viewpoints. A social nature predisposes one to encounters with others and therefore raises the

8

likelihood that learning can occur. The advent of the Internet is especially salient, as the Internet allows individuals from radically different cultures, religions, and political affiliations to congregate together in a virtual public square and to communicate together in ways never before possible. In this new age, where knowledge is currency and power, one with broad social interactions only gains a learning advantage.

3. Social Interaction Boosts Longevity

Quality social interactions promote long life.[6] Fun times with family, friends and others alleviate stress. Alleviation of stress leads to a reduction of illness such as cardiovascular disease, cancer and high blood pressure. Studies also show that social interaction boosts the immune system and keeps lesser evils like flu and colds at bay. Since illness is a major cause of unhappiness, its absence implies an increase possibility of greater happiness.

4. Social Interaction Enhances Self-Esteem

Early social interaction lays the groundwork for the development of self-esteem. In early childhood, repeated social interaction reinforces appropriate behaviors such as respect, ability to work in small groups, and sharing.[7] These skills retain value well-past the playground years and translate to acceptance in society. Acceptance in society leads to success in the workplace and educational environments where collaborative effort is the norm, and—when sustained—this success boosts life-long self-esteem.

5. Social Interaction Keeps the 'Golden Years' Golden

The arrival of newer and better medical technologies assures that many more people live longer lives. At first glance, there would seem to be no downside to living well into the 70s, 80s, and 90s and beyond. However, the specter of Alzheimer's and similar diseases loom over today's seniors. Memory loss and more general mental deterioration terrifies people and tempers later life with fears of dying old, alone and mentally incompetent. Fortunately, social interaction appears to ward off Alzheimer's-like diseases and related depression, leading to real happiness in the elderly.[8]

6. Social Interaction Produces Positive Memories

Social interaction does not simply function to keep memories intact. Social interaction leads to the formation of positive memories all throughout life. Persons who use their social graces to cultivate strong family, friend and romantic bonds, can look back on life and bask in memories associated with those bonds. Rather than catalog endless regrets, an interactive person's mind will forever house the memories of blissful Thanksgiving dinners with family, childhood adventures, and romantic dalliances. A head filled with such memories is a happy head indeed.

7. Social Interaction Drives Altruism

The skills that social interaction hones are the same skills that fuel feelings of altruism.[9] Altruism is the pursuit of a greater good that extends beyond any immediate benefit to one's self. Reciprocity and similar behaviors can advance beyond simple 'give and take' and lead one to give without expecting anything in return. Persons who exude altruism delight and inspire others around them with their gracious and self-less overtures. This benefits society directly and indirectly fosters esteem and satisfaction in the altruist. All are happy and all win in an environment in which altruism is the predominant spirit.

What is Social Anxiety and How Do You Conquer It?

The ubiquity of all things social in modern times forces one to confront the dark side of social interaction. Twenty-first century society does not consist of social butterflies with gilded tongues and graces envious of Emily Post. Social interaction is something to be feared and avoided at all costs by wide swathes of society. Why, one might ask. The answer is simple. A significant number of people suffer from social anxiety. In fact, the American Psychological Association declares social anxiety to be the third largest mental health care issue interfering with the lives of millions, and it sits squarely behind depression and alcoholism in its prevalence.[10]

Social anxiety is neither jitters at the prospect of a job interview nor fear of alienating a new romantic prospect on a first date. Social anxiety is an all-pervasive dread surrounding the very idea of interacting with others. Persons suffering from this disorder are inordinately self-conscious and feel as though a giant spotlight of negative judgment and derision ceaselessly shines down upon them.[10] The threat of public speaking, chance meetings with strangers, social introductions to authority figures and similar forced gatherings is soul crushing. While so engrossed with intrusive thoughts touting the humiliation that is likely to come, their very bodies may begin to betray them. Persons in the vicinity may peg social anxiety suffers as nervous nellies who are markedly uncomfortable in the environment in which they find themselves. Inwardly, persons with social anxiety may experience accelerated pulses, intense fear, nausea, and a dry mouth. If the feelings persist unabated, such persons may begin to shake, twitch and/or perspire profusely.[10] Social anxiety is serious and something to be mindful of in today's society.

No one wants to suffer with social anxiety. The socially anxious person is no exception and would gladly be the 'likeable' person discussed in sections to follow, but this is easier said than done. Such persons tend to know that their fears are irrational, but they are held hostage by them nevertheless. This problem is compounded by the fact that the top minds in brain science are not 100% certain as to the cause of generalized anxiety disorders. Thus, there is no 'silver bullet' that can magically and irrevocably quell all cases of social anxiety in all persons. At present there are a mélange of theories, drugs and therapies that may or may not work. Nonetheless, scientists agree that the disorder is likely to be inherited. Further, the origin of the condition may lie within the amygdala.[11] The amygdala is a tiny structure deep within the recesses of the human 'reptile' brain, and it is responsible for the primitive 'fight, flight or freeze' response that is elicited by humans in the face of threats. A faulty amygdala stuck in fear mode is consequently one model used to explain the phenomenon. Other theories revolve around environment. Persons who have suffered immense childhood tragedies and wildly unstable, familial homes may see their early fears persisted throughout a lifetime. Fortunately, a combination of anti-depressants, cognitive therapy and exposure therapy have proven efficacy in combatting the problem.

What are the 5 Key Types of Social Interactions?

When it comes to the social realm, one must not assume that all interactions eventuate in 'rainbows and butterflies,' feel-good, honest exchanges amongst parties. Social interaction is generally a positive facet of humanity. However, some interactions are colored by an ambiguity or complexity that puts their value in question. The positive and negative aspects of social interaction are born out in the works of esteemed sociologist Robert Nisbet. Nisbet's core focus was the growth of communities, and an offshoot of his work addresses five types of social interactions that eventuate amongst individuals, groups and societies as a whole.[12] These interactions are detailed below –

1. Cooperation

Cooperation is the very glue of society, and it comprises collectives of individuals working together

17

to achieve a goal that is perceived by them to be beneficial to all. The innate drive for cooperation runs strong and deep and is the impulse that allowed early man to form primitive societies. Still, basic tribal cooperation has been superseded by more modern forms which deviate from a straight-forward 'one for all and all for one' mentality. In modern times, cooperation is more likely to center on a single authority figure who offers some monetary or power exchange for the express cooperation of his underlings. A prime example would be employees who cooperate with an unlikeable boss for the express purpose of earning a paycheck. Likewise, contracted cooperation characterizes groups of individuals who agree to combine forces only around one central need. The oft cited example of this latter form of cooperation is groups of mothers who only come together and pool resources to ensure that babysitting needs are met. Thus, cooperation may be a purely altruistic endeavor or it may be a euphemism for various models of mutual utilization.

2. Competition

Competition has evolved with both negative and positive connotations, and Nisbet's work attests to both facets of the phenomenon. Competition understood in the simplest terms is a form of cooperation that puts willing participants together to achieve some goal deemed to be desirable to all. In its most positive manifestations, the participants focus energy away from competitors and on the goal itself. For example, think of U.S. Olympic contenders performing their personal best to ensure a spot on the national team. While these athletes put their personal bests against one another, their shared desire is the acquisition of a gold medal for the United States. In its negative manifestations, competitors lose sight of the goal and engage in overt conflict with one another. This latter possibility must be prevented at all costs to elicit any value from competition, and the way to guard against devolution into hostile, aggressive feelings and actions is to ensure that clear 'rules of engagement' are enforced. With that said, conflict will be briefly revisited as a third social interaction style in the topic to follow.

3. Conflict

The negative aspects of conflict were touched upon briefly above. The dark side of the phenomenon is apt to be understood by most readers, so the subject will not be delved into further. However, suffice it to say that conflicts are not without potential benefits. While inter-group fighting can have a deleterious effect on the social whole, external threats can actually bring groups together. Whereas ethnic infighting may ravage a country with petty skirmishes, these same groups of opposed people may form together to stave off a grave threat compromising the country as a whole. Thus, conflict in various forms can promote positive interaction, albeit indirectly.

4. Social Exchange

Social Exchange in its most blunt form is one individual, group or society performing in such a way as to reap benefits from another individual, group or society. Blatant examples of social exchange would be politicians kissing babies for votes or wait staff disingenuously pandering to customers for inflated tips. Less obvious forms of exchange are niceties such as a quick wave or other social greeting. While such behaviors may seem innocuous and likely to be brushed off if not reciprocated, unrequited politeness may evoke feelings of anger or disappointment when not received.

5. Coercion

Coercion is forced group interaction that is thrust upon one by some outside source or dictatorial authority.

Hapless political prisoners thrust together in work camps—attended to by armed guards—are an obvious example of coercion. However, far more subtle forms exist. Employees who drag their feet on their way to boring or unproductive meetings may be said to be coerced, if their attendance arises from fear of job loss, managerial retribution or damaging workplace gossip.

What Makes People Likeable?

How does one become likeable? The answer to this question seems apt to evade one much like 'why is there something rather than nothing?' Is there any way in which such a broad question pertaining to a mysterious attribute be answered? One may not think so. Nevertheless, psychologists and social theorists have tackled the phenomenon and have jointly settled on several traits at the core of 'likeability.'[13]

First, likeable people wear their sense of security in the world like a badge. Likeable people are not the proverbial wall-flowers who wilt and shirk at the thought of public exposure. Likeable people stride into the room with the air of confidence enveloping them like a pleasant perfume. While wall-flowers and other shrinking violets may have genuinely admirable traits, they may never be known, because their perennial insecurities and resultant lack of action prevent them from showcasing other more admirable traits.

23

Likeable people may stride into a room as if they are 'all that and then some,' but their attitude is forever humble. Their egos are not as palpable as their confidence. They do not judge others who lack their own finesse. They do not judge people who differ from them in social standing, worldview or other characteristics. Instead, likeable people radiate approachability, and this is a big secret to their social success. They are approachable when so many people are not, and this approachability draws people in for the potential of extended interaction.

The likeable person is 'real.' They are not perpetrating an act on society. This is not successful or advanced 'posing.' To be likeable, one must be authentic in one's social interactions. One must genuinely thrive on quality interaction, and this entails a stance of care and concern for those who gamely approach. Care and concern is further evidenced by active listening and a willingness to know and understand one's interlocutors rather than simply use one's contacts to advance one's own interests or bring attention to accomplishments. Any person who presents themselves without this innate care and concern will undoubtedly be unsuccessful in social endeavors, as their veneer is likely to crack under the weight of an unsustainable falsehood.

Likeable people know that the most effective means to capitalize on interaction is to skip negative ruminations; petty gossip and 'weather' talk and direct their conversational prowess towards things that matter. Titillating gossip and conversations centered on 'snowpocalypses' and other weather sensations have their time and place. They may be quick icebreakers and bring comic or other relief to lackluster or floundering interactions. However, there is no longevity to be had in such a conversation. Negativity is never appealing and should be avoided at all costs. In today's parlance 'Debbie Downers' are patently unwelcome in most social spheres. Likeable people simply do not bring down a conversation to its knees through relentless bemoaning of the state of things. They uplift their audience by asking appropriately intimate questions about their partner-in-speech's every day wants, needs and desires. They tune into their partner, make their partner feel valued, laud their partner's achievements and give that partner every opportunity to contribute in a way that is suitable to his or her level of social interaction.

Finally, what happens when a likeable person meets an unlikeable person? Is it akin to an irresistible force meeting an unmovable object? On the contrary, the likeable person realizes that the unlikeable person may be suffering a depressed mood stemming from adverse life circumstances. The likeable person knows that they have been no stranger to such circumstances and have had less than perfect behavior, so they give the unlikeable person the benefit of the doubt and further chances for improved interaction.

Case Study #1: Abraham Lincoln

Since time immemorial, tiny children have learned about 'Honest Abe.' Older children know him as the celebrated freer of slaves and author of the Gettysburg Address. By college, students may be conversant with wife Mary Todd Lincoln's alleged mental illness. However, what of Abe himself? While Lincoln cuts a very stern looking figure in extant photos, few associate him with any sort of mental or emotional impediment. Nevertheless, research suggests that Abraham Lincoln had a predisposition to anxiety or depression which cast a pall on his personal life.[14] While Lincoln undoubtedly suffered, his towering achievements as a state leader and politician speak to his ability to transform personal pain into depth of feeling, empathy and an uncanny ability to connect to others. Consequently, Lincoln's overall likeability and finesse for social interaction is remembered to this day.

Lincoln clearly experienced overwhelming trauma and uncertainty in his early years.[14] He was born into a poor farming family in rural Kentucky. His mother succumbed to a kind of food poisoning when Lincoln was 9, causing his distant father to temporarily abandon the family in search of a new matriarch. His beloved sister died during child birth. Later, 8 of Lincoln's own 10 children would die prematurely. This lifetime of profound losses and an absent father undoubtedly left Lincoln scarred. This was compounded by insecurities that Lincoln felt as an uneducated man of low birth trying to navigate his way through elite society. Fortunately, Lincoln's story did not die out in the backwoods of Kentucky. Instead, Lincoln appears to have exercised innate, interpersonal skills to great advantage; skills like those lauded by more modern, personal success gurus Dale Carnegie and Napoleon Hill.

Lincoln is not known to have a sunny disposition. Nevertheless, some part of him accorded the vision and inner strength needed to self-educate in the field of law. This positive and patient drive catapulted him from a stint in the court room to the U.S. House of Representatives and on to the presidency itself. It was in this role as POTUS (President of the United States) that Abraham Lincoln's true skills as a leader were fully actualized. Testimony of Lincoln's abilities abound. However, his treatment of the soldiers of the Army of the Potomac speaks volumes.[15] These were the soldiers that fought at famed and bloody battles such as Bull Run, Fredericksburg and Gettysburg. Rather than eschew the field of battle for the safety of the White House, Lincoln rode out into the fields to uplift the spirits of these men and to actively listen as they recounted their harrowing experiences. He made the men feel important, no matter what their rank. Everyone who wanted an audience was welcome to speak. This accessibility extended well beyond the battlefield. He and his wife bestowed further kindness by sitting at the bedsides of wounded soldiers, and the couple entertained men in the White House, as well. Lincoln even 'self-edited' the themes of his speeches so that soldiers were not off-put by new ideas like emancipation. Instead, they slowly warmed to them over time. Lincoln's leadership charisma was so great that even ambivalent or opposed Union soldiers would write home to proclaim that Lincoln's ideas of freedom, justice and equality had become their own, heartfelt battle cries. This is the hallmark of a great leader.

And what of Lincoln's anxiety issue? Far from a handicap, his melancholic countenance was viewed by men as an outward expression of his grave concern for them and his shared humanity. It caused them to reciprocate deep feeling for him, and this visible authenticity earned him the "Honest Abe" moniker.

Persons suffering from anxiety in modern times should learn that there are no limits in life and anyone can become likable and a master of social interaction.

Case Study #2: Warren Buffett

Warren Buffet is a 'mover and shaker' commanding unimaginable wealth and power. Buffett is the uncontested top investor of the twentieth century, and he vies for the position of wealthiest man on Earth. Buffet is variably described as a magnate, billionaire investor and philanthropist, and he is the bearer of the whimsical moniker "the Wizard of Omaha." Surely, Warren Buffet is not cut from the same cloth as any average Joe. Or, is he?

Mere mortals are not likely to find immediate affinity with Warren Buffet. He seems larger than life and well removed from any issues that confront ordinary individuals in their everyday lives. However, Warren Buffett shares many commonalities with everyday folk, and he likes it that way. First, unlike many men of his stature, Buffett chooses not to make NYC his home. He does not live in sunny California, either. Instead, Buffett chooses to stay in homely Omaha,

Nebraska. He has neither a multi-million dollar home nor a yacht. Instead, he comfortably lives in a home he bought decades ago for $31,000. Buffett even heralds the idea that others among his class swear off ostentatious and wasteful living and give back to their communities through the means of higher taxes or charity. Buffett's frugal lifestyle is an admirable choice.[16] However, he shares another similarity with millions of people that are not of his own choosing. Buffett is affected with social anxiety disorder.[17]

Long before Buffett became a billionaire, he was but a young man with an overwhelming fear of public speaking. Buffet was so fearful of the prospect of speaking before his peers, that he painstakingly organized college classes in such a way as to avoid presenting speeches. By and by, he realized that this fear could only hold him back, so he endeavored to confront and conquer his fear by enrolling himself in a public speaking class. The urge to challenge himself quickly vanquished. His apprehension returned, and he exempted himself from the class, before it even began.

Buffet went on to enjoy his future successes, but the notion persisted that his inability to address public audiences was an impediment to his growth potential. Though public speaking quite literally made him ill, he steeled himself and joined a Dale Carnegie class scoped to individuals suffering from the same condition that limited him all his life. This course gave him the outlook and the tools needed to put his anxiety issue behind him. He learned the value of confronting fears. He learned proper use of praise to engage people and to motivate them. He also learned to never criticize them. His efforts paid off. Not only did he cement himself in history as one of the world's greatest managers, he went on to give many lectures, speeches and interviews. Most notably, Warren has addressed many college business students including, but not exclusive to, Tuck, Vanderbilt and Wharton students. Buffett perceives these engagements as yet another means to give back by encouraging others to step outside their comfort zones and release their full potential.

Today, Buffett's Carnegie class certificate is alleged to hang framed on his office wall as a lasting testament to the importance of his achievement.[18] Buffet himself states that his hard-one ability to communicate effectively is one of the key factors in his immeasurable success. As he sees it, failure to hone this skill entails that one sells one's self short. Readers should consider this a lesson learned. Actors, musicians, politicians and other star players on the world stage have or continue to suffer from social anxiety. However, with the right attitude, proper training and other recourses, it can be overcome and a 'wealth' of opportunities opens up! Just ask Warren Buffett.

7 Steps to Starting and Holding a Conversation

How does one progress from tripping over one's own tongue to attaining the status of world-class conversationalist? The road may be long, but there are clearly delineated steps that anyone can take down that road to realize a future of speaking with ease. The following steps are tried and true means to get there –

1. Embrace Fear

The fear of addressing individuals or groups of individuals is very real. To conquer that fear, embrace it for what it is, realize that you are not alone in this fear, and opt to move beyond it. Many persons functioning at all levels of society have known the trepidation involved in giving voice to one's thoughts in front of an audience. However, many people have moved beyond it. It is a doable proposition.

2. Embrace an "As If" Attitude

You may be shaking in your boots, but the world does not need to know this. Therefore, employ the 'As If' technique to compensate for the security that you lack in the face of public speaking.[19] To effectively operate in 'As If' mode, study the characteristics of successful speakers. Take note of modes of dress, gesturing, eye contact and phrasing used. Keep mental notes in hand and practice what you have seen. With this method, you do not want to be a poser slipping into an unnatural, ill-fitting, 'skin' devoid of resemblance to yourself. Instead, develop a comfortable persona of your own, one that incorporates a blending of your own true self with desired traits exhibited by your role model. Thus, you will be able to act 'as if' you came stocked with the desired traits when the time is right.

3. Develop Conversation Starters

A mental cache of conversation starters is a must for individuals who need a predefined sense of control and progression in a conversation. Persons dreading sports may flounder, if a potential conversation partner launches into an impromptu, play-by-play discussion of last night's big game. Unemployed persons may experience horror and humiliation when the topics of career trajectories, storied salaries and big promotions pop up unexpectedly at a dinner party. To avoid your own flubs and frustrations, arm yourself with 'starters' appropriate to the context in which potential conversations may occur. If you love alternative music, innocuously seek opinions of a new Indie star when attending popular concerts. If you are a foodie, steal the dinner party by critiquing the new restaurant on the block and sharing family recipes. These starters give you a leg up on the conversation by bestowing control and are sure to encounter other parties with like interests.

4. Go to the Action

You are not likely to find stellar conversation in the confines of your own living room. Instead, you must amass gumption and put yourself out in environments where you are likely to find persons with whom to speak. Loud Rock concerts and movies are not appropriate venues. Coffee shops, some bookstores, hobbyist meet ups and the like are appropriate venues, in which you are likely to find agreeable persons with whom you can apply your skills.

5. Remember Conversation is a Two-Way Proposition

Conversation starters are great, especially when combined with venues where parties are willing to engage in such preconceived talk. However, conversation is not unidirectional. Be prepared for surprises. The single father at the art opening may care more about last night's Big Game than any painting hanging on the wall. The dedicated foodie may want to divert talk away from the block's new bistro to talk of the day's top news story. Be flexible. Be prepared. And, when talk does not progress smoothly, use the opportunity to query the speaker about his or her interests, employ active listening skills and enjoy the conversation!

6. Use Humor

Humor is the saving grace of many conversations. If the subject matter drifts into sticky political or religious talk, a humorous exit strategy may be warranted. If you let slip an awkward phrase or opinion, you may resort to humor to diffuse any offense or embarrassment. If you are not naturally inclined to one-liners or other witty quips, you may choose to fall back on light talk pertaining to funny internet memes or cat pictures.

7. Know When to Quit

Good conversation is an art form much like cooking or painting. Therefore, skills are needed to assess when the work is done and when one should step away. This may not be obvious to the new conversationalist. Still, it can be learned with time and experience. Newbies should pick up a good book on body language, as body language provides the most reliable queues. Polite persons may feign interest in a deathless conversation for the sake of politeness. However, body language belies an audience's true feelings. Failing eye-contact, increased distance, closed postures, yawning and other queues signal the flagging commitment of the conversation partner. Do the right thing and bow out, and more conversations may be had in the future!

21 Ways to Connect with Anyone, Anywhere

Connection starts with conversation. However, conversation is only a vehicle through which the meaningful exchange of ideas can occur. Real connection comes from shared worldviews, insights and emotions. To connect on this level, employ the following strategies as opportunity allows –

1. Frequent Venues that Promote Interaction

Cinemas are not a valid option for anyone who wants to interact with others in an in-depth manner. Deep conversation cannot burgeon in any environment where the mere act of speech is considered a major faux pas punishable by death. (Try carrying on an extended conversation during a major blockbuster and see what happens!) Spare yourself the dirty looks, and go to venues where people want to interact with others.

2. Paint a Mental Picture of the Person You Want Proceed Accordingly

Don't go to biker bars or sporting events, if you want to meet people who share your love of coin collecting. Sure, the president of the local numismatics society might ride a Harley and moonlight as a bona fide sports jock. However, a more fitting first step might be a leisurely trip to a flea market where coin collectors congregate. Make connecting easy and straight-forward!

3. Arrive on Scene with Confidence

Looking dazed and confused while slinking about or worse—hugging the wall—does nothing for your image. It makes you unapproachable. Unapproachable people do not connect with anyone. They go home alone, defeated. Spare yourself the disappointment. Put on your game face and stride into the room with confidence and command the scene.

4. Remember that New People Are Unaware of Your Fears and Foibles

The stranger across the crowded room does not know that you are deathly self-conscious about your receding hairline or expanded girth. They don't know that you are shaking in your boots at the thought of encounters with strangers, unless of course, you are visibly shaking! If confidence is not native to your constitution, handle stranger encounters with the 'as-if' concept and wear confidence as your middle name (see above).

5. Start the Conversation

The person to whom you take an interest might have their own social interaction issues. Be proactive and break the ice. Someone needs to do it, and failure to connect on the part of both parties may lead to loss of a future partner, job or big sale. Think big and take the risk.

6. Tailor Your Conversation to Your Audience

Once you find like-minded individuals, customize your conversation around any shared interests. Anyone can conduct small-talk. However, rehashing of weather-related observations or tired celebrity news does nothing to deepen conversations or connections. Don't hem and haw over unseasonable temperatures when you can share your passion for social justice or environmentalism with like-minded people. Be bold and discuss issues and interests of real concern to you both.

7. Avoid Jargon-Laden Speech

Overuse of buzzwords is off-putting. You won't connect to anyone other than sales people if your audience has to engage in mental gymnastics to interpret everything you say. Connection is communicating and communicating in bizarre, inappropriate, and inscrutable phrases is antithetical to your endeavor.

8. 'Vision-Paint' a Shared Reality

Admittedly, 'vision painting' is one of those verboten buzzwords! However, vision painting has a certain romance and utility to it not characteristic of other words in this genre. Vision painting entails construction of a shared, future reality based on observations, attitudes and desires about the present day. If you and your conversation partner are equally bothered by the crumbling state of your community, muse about a world in which you both take action, motivate others to do the same and bring about real change.

9. Show Enthusiasm

Show appropriate excitement whether you are vision painting or conversing in any other manner. To do so lends an air of vitality to the conversation that might ignite a deeper connection.

10. Listen

You cannot possibly hope to connect with another individual, if you do not pay attention to what the other person says. Employ active listening techniques for best results. Active listening and repetition of the words your conversation partner uses allows for confirmation that one has been heard correctly. There is no better way to demonstrate attentiveness to another person than active listening.

11. Demonstrate Empathy

Persons want to be heard. More importantly, they want their experiences to be validated. Unlike sympathy, empathy is more than a quick nod or understanding words. Empathy is an acknowledgement that you share someone else's pain, because you too have lived it. Application of empathy is particularly important when conversing with one who has suffered tragedy or other setbacks in life. Don't ring hollow. Step up and relate by sharing your own adversities.

12. Make Eye Contact

The role that eye contact plays in human connection cannot be overstated. In Western society, appropriate eye contact conveys respect. To look into another's eyes is to communicate that one feels equal to another. It also conveys interest and understanding. Failure to look into another's eyes lends an air of aloofness to social interaction. It signals to another that what they have to say is unimportant.

13. Exploit Body Language in General

Body language is a comprehensive subject fit to be studied by anyone wanting to promote interpersonal connections. Start small. Maintain open posture at all times, lean in and tilt your head subtly to the side to signal engagement.

14. Help a Person Out

It can't be stressed enough, that a wide segment of the population has issues with social interaction, often due to anxiety or introversion. Such people may easily become intimidated by the idea of communicating with others. Should they venture out to do so, they may find themselves in situations in which they are hurt, criticized or ignored by others who sense their insecurities and inappropriate actions. Come to the rescue of such people, and you are apt to establish an immediate connection.

15.   Create Your Own Opportunities

Not all strangers linger alone across a crowded room. You may find that many persons of interest are actively engaged in conversations with others. Do not miss the opportunity. While it is rude to brusquely insert one's self into a conversation, use the situation to your advantage. If you walk by and inadvertently overhear the person express an interest similar to your own, make a note. Then, when the time is right, approach the interesting stranger and lead in with, "I couldn't help but over hearing…." Then, promote an immediate bond by revealing your shared interest.

16.   Exploit Technology

Meet ups and forums, dating services and other online venues make it easy to find that person who is looking for someone exactly like you.

17.   Be Open to a Range of Possibilities

Let's face it. Finding others who share your love of Ethiopian cuisine or medieval choral music may be difficult. Make the best effort. However, you may need to broaden your horizons. Do not assume that people who do not share such interests cannot connect to you. A person who has an unusual interest in Gnawa music—which you may never have heard of—may be game for trying your Ethiopian food. Someone who loves period literature may not have heard medieval music before, but it may intrigue them nonetheless.

Use differences in life to broaden others' interests and learn new things yourself.

18.   Find Value in All Your Relationship

Some people may not share any of your interests ever. Some may dramatically differ from you in culture, religion, politics or socio-economic status. You may see other people only as coworkers, customers or service providers, devoid of connection potential. However, these seemingly trivial and tenuous connections can flourish into burgeoning friendships or romances, if valued properly and explored. Lead with a gracious demeanor, ask questions about their world views and experiences, listen and learn, and see where it goes.

19.   Delight Unsuspecting Individuals

Upper management, business prospects and romantic interests expect to be treated with respect. However, service industry providers or abject strangers may not.

Even though such individuals may provoke no immediate interest in you, wow them with novel interest taking, care and concern. Underappreciated persons will usually respond with surprise and appreciation. This could initiate the unfolding of a friendship or romance, or it could simply seal your reputation as a highly likeable person. Connections of either depth are just fine.

20. Confide in Others

If you reveal your own vulnerabilities to others, they may reciprocate. It is only when persons are fully authentic and open that the deepest connections can occur.

21. Practice Judiciously

Social interaction is hard for some and easy for others. However, no matter what your proficiency level, practice, practice, practice.

14 Actionable Tips to Becoming More Likeable

'Personal Success' theorist and author Napoleon Hill wrote the veritable bible on likeability. Hill titles such as, *Think and Grow Rich,* are more than feel good, self-help pabulums designed to rob a gullible public of the cost of a book. Instead, this and other books in his oeuvre break down the development of personal amiability and success into individual action items and present them as a science. But who is Napoleon Hill, and why should one lend any credence to his philosophy?

Napoleon Hill was born in 1883. Though not a contemporary of Abraham Lincoln, he shares some of the elder man's daunting life experiences.[20]

He was raised in a humble cabin in rural Virginia. He suffered the premature death of his mother at age nine. Somehow, he maintained a sense of ambition which saw him secure employment as a reporter at the tender age of thirteen. While Hill would work a rural beat for many years, the story does not end there. A 'big break' occurred in 1908, which catapulted Hill into fame that outlasts him to this day.[20]

The assignment was simple. Hill was to interview successful and famous men. The purpose of the interviews was to provide copy for a series of articles on the lives of these men. Hill commenced with an interview of Andrew Carnegie and then rolled through A-level contacts, which Carnegie graciously provided. The result was far more than interview copy. Instead, Hill capsulized the men's stellar success into checklists that the common man could use to achieve the same results, and that checklist is still relevant to this day.

What follows is a series of paraphrased points with added examples, based on Hill's work "Develop a Pleasing Personality."[21] Persons wanting to be pleasing or 'likeable' should conceive this list as a set of action items to be practiced on a daily basis.

1. Never Underestimate the Value of Positivity

Attitude is everything. In order to succeed, one must divest one's self of negative thought patterns and exude positivity in anything that one does. Negativity only begets negativity. Criticism is to be especially avoided as this form of negativity is self-destructive and dampens one's reputation. Positivity—on the other hand—is infectious and causes those around one to drink in a pleasing vibe and to associate that vibe with the positive person. Hence, persons forever seek out the positive person's attention.

2. Adopt a Stance of Active Listening

Overt egoism is just as detrimental as negativity. Persons, who are made to feel snubbed, ignored or generally unimportant do not want to be around people who make them feel that way. To avoid off-putting a target audience, the likeable person listens deeply and with intent. They validate their opinion and welcome their contributions.

3. Make People Feel Important

In fact, make people feel like they are the most important person in the room. This is not hyperbole. In today's society, it is commonplace for persons to find their thoughts and feelings brushed aside by inconsiderate people who are more attentive to the latest cellphone calls, text messages or Facebook media posts that—in today's parlance—'blow up' their phones. A person who forgoes interruptions caused by phones, ambient conversations, TVs and other distractions is a rarity and relief. These people make one feel important and are instantly likeable.

4. Be Open

Likeability does not stop with listening and conceding to other's views. It is optimally important that the likeable person maintain a truly open mind. This speaks to authenticity. One should not bow to others to win their vote of approval. Instead, one must strive to truly understand and embrace—where possible—the ideas of those who differ from him or her.

5. Smile

Smiling is more than a cultural nicety. Smiling actually triggers a neurochemical response in the brain that enhances one's mood. The benefits do not stop there. Persons who smile elicit the same reactions in others and can even make one appear more physically attractive. Smiling is so important that customer service managers and others encourage employees to smile when talking to contacts on the phone.

6. Be Easy on the Ears

Voice quality is just as important as mental attitude and a friendly face. Tremulous, raucous or whiny voices are hard on the ear. If one is going to commit to cultivating likeability, one must devote equal time to cultivating a strong and confident voice with warm undertones. Such voices are persuasive and seductive and have mileage in both work and social milieus.

7. Self-Edit

Nothing can be gained from letting uncharitable thoughts slip past one's stream of consciousness and out through one's mouth. There is no case to be made for offending people. Deliberate or inadvertent offensive statements create distance in the hearer and prevent that hearer from maintaining his or her own open mind. They also cannot be unheard. When in doubt, one should not say it.

8. Remain Calm

Likeable people are not reactionary. Let's face it. Other people will do and say things that rile one's soul. Employees may laugh at a new manager's performance analysis. Children may be verbally disrespectful to their parents. A romantic prospect may use the 'let's be friends' line. These things happen. However, the likeable person does not let sudden emotion spill over into reaction. Storming out of rooms, slamming doors or returning insults does not advance likeability. Instead, it puts one off one's game and causes one to behave in ways that promote further disdain in the audience. Likeable people maintain a calm and collected stance, mull over the adverse situation and plan a win-back scenario to everyone's delight.

9. Do Not Procrastinate

A copywriter who misses deadlines does not garner praise. The missed deadline may appear trivial. However, that act of procrastination may cause upper management to rain down hellfire and brimstone on the copywriter's own manager. This condemnation will be forever burned in the mind of the manager and associated with the lax writer. Likeable people realize that their own actions may reflect on others and affect others in ways that are not obvious. Therefore, likeable people always meet their obligations in a timely fashion.

10.   Remember that Patience is a Virtue

Whereas procrastination is bad, it is equally bad to rush through endeavors without regard to timing. Romantic partners may have a general interest in one. However, work deadlines, ailing parent issues or childcare matters may make it inopportune to rush off on a coveted three day weekend. Likeable people do not force the issue. They know that a perceived lack of concern for another's commitments may translate to feelings of disrespect in that other person. Worse, the reluctant partner who concedes and goes along on the badly timed outing may feel as if they are doing so out of duress.

11. Be Kind

Acts of kindness seal the likeable person's reputation in the hearts and minds of act recipients. The employed friend who provides industry contacts and job leads to an unemployed associate is a hero. People like heroes.

12. Praise Others

Praise is the simplest act of kindness that buoys people's spirits. The instructor who praises the struggling student's honest efforts may be the highlight of that student's career. Likeable people use praise to their advantage and bestow authentic praise when praise is warranted.

13. Practice Self-Improvement

Likeable does not equate to perfect. Likeable people know that they are not perfect. To secure their status, likeable people engage confidants to point out critical flaws. Then, they create their own action item list to rectify those flaws. Interviewees with closed body language or singles who have a tendency to interrupt conversation would benefit from this type of likeability coaching.

14. See Success

Likeable people don't see failures. They only see learning experiences and teachable moments. No one succeeds 100% of the time. Likeable people do not allow failures to pitch them into negativity, thereby denting their amiable stance. They are true, unflappable thought leaders who soldier through difficulties, learn lessons that allow them to succeed in future endeavors, and teach others the secrets to their tenacity. Thus completing Napoleon Hill's fourteen steps would ensure likeability. But what of the fifteenth?

Napoleon Hill has been credited with stating, "Anything the mind of man can conceive and believe, it can be achieved."[22] Though not an action item per se, it is a guiding principle that one should keep foremost in mind when embarking on a personal growth project or any other endeavor of this importance. Anything is possible with the right mindset and effort.

How to Continue Conversations after the First Meeting Ends

In the best of all possible worlds, one scintillating dinner conversation should lead to another and another. The inspired elevator speech should lead to a million dollar deal. However, there are no guarantees. The master of social interaction is saliently aware that continued conversation requires diligent and tactful follow-up. Though scenarios may differ, there are steps that anyone can take to better ensure that their first conversation is not the last. These tips and tricks come from the sales and interview world, but they can be tailored to any situation.[23]

1. Create Your Opportunity

Ensure that your first conversation leads off with an entrée point for a second conversation. If your date expresses passing enthusiasm for an upcoming event, take note. An invite to the mentioned event could be a great second conversation starter and a pleasant surprise. If a business prospect expresses interest in a certain feature not realized in current products, take note. If product management confirms the presence of the feature in your own product line, this would be a very legitimate reason to call the prospect back.

2. Exercise Patience

Wait two to three days before calling the individual for a follow-up conversation. Romantic interests, hiring managers and business managers have at least one thing in common. They do not want to be hounded by someone they perceive to be desperate. Desperate behavior undercuts legitimacy. You want your date to believe that they are <u>that</u> someone special. You want hiring managers to know that you are the ideal candidate. You want business partners to realize that you have the singular solution to solve all of their pain points. You do not want these people to feel that they are 'any port in the storm,' and too soon calling risks communicating this message.

3. Beware of the 'Gatekeeper'

In business and hiring situations, receptionists might claim that 'so-and-so is' in a meeting. That person may well be in a meeting. That person may be avoiding your call. Alternatively, the receptionist may simply assume that you are a pest to be brushed off, like so many others. Ask the receptionist to pin down a time when the callee may be available and await for the appointed hour. If the target does not honor the call after one or two subsequent follow-ups, then it may be the case that no second conversation is in order. Send a follow-up email to the intended individual and see if they respond. If nothing is forthcoming, it is best to let the matter rest. Dating is somewhat different. If your romantic partner's phone consistently rings through to a roommate or other unanticipated person, your date is likely not interested. If they are interested, they will likely follow-up on their own on or before the conventional three-day waiting period has passed.

4. Avoid the 'Hard Sell'

It is wrong to demand that a person date you simply because you think you are perfect and likely to be scooped up at a moment's notice. That is a 'ginormous' red flag, and sensible people are right not to date you. Hiring managers and business prospects expect this sort of thing. However, be delightfully different in all business interactions. In hiring situations, forgo the obvious question, 'Did I get the job?' When business deals are on the line, avoid abrupt talk of deal closings. Instead, lead in with some pithy insight that you have arrived at concerning the company or industry at large. Position the insight in such a way as to intrigue the listener and make them think or question. Are you at a loss for ideas? Well, a business prospect may be excited to hear how an unknown niche industry may be a prime target for their startup products. The hiring manager may be interested to hear about localization or personalization ideas that you arrived at while browsing the company's end user portal.

5. Create Value

Remember that business situations demand a clear delineation of value proposition. Don't just sell yourself or your product. Ensure that a burgeoning, second conversation includes talk of why you or your product will cut costs, raise revenues or revolutionize the product line. 'Value proposition' may not be a concept bandied about the dating world. However, a second conversation should contain some talk of your shared lifestyles, views and aspirations. This tells your date that you might add value to their life.

Utilize the above tips and tricks, and you may be well on your way to a third conversation!

How to Maintain Authentic Relationships in Your Life

Virtually everyone has some conception of what a relationship is, and most people understand that there are a wide variety of relationship types. Relationships of the boy-meets-girl kind are easily juxtaposed with familial and business relationships. Almost everyone knows intuitively—if not intellectually—what the benefits of relationships happen to be. Relationships, simply put, tend to be the prime drivers of satisfaction in life. However, many people do not know that relationships have life cycles.[24] Whereas the concept of a life cycle is more readily familiar to children studying frogs, chickens and bean sprouts, it may be less apparent to adults to apply the same concept to each and every one of their own relationships.

Why should one take the time to apprise themselves of theories of relationship lifecycles? Yes, there are theories in the plural. There is not one, all-encompassing viewpoint. The answer is still simple. People generally want to maintain their relationships. Failed relationships equate to loss of satisfaction, and nobody wants that. Today's divorce rate alone bears ample witness to the notion that adults do not proactively understand the evolution and devolution of interpersonal relationships. Dysfunctional families combined with workplace and school violence further supports the premise that something is wrong. Fortunately, one does not need to pursue advanced degrees in sociology or psychology to solve the problems latent or blatant in one's own relationship life. One simply needs to learn basic principles to better the odds that encourage established relationships to remain in bloom, much like the plants children plant in their early life sciences classes.

To continue the apt plant metaphor, relationships need to be nurtured and maintained at each juncture from the time they come into being, until the time they die natural or slow agonizing deaths. The plant metaphor only goes so far, so this line of argumentation will need to continue without recourse to our green, leafy friends. Basically, the start of a relationship can be properly conceived of as its initiating stage or event. This event can be a chance meeting across a crowded room or a job interview. If pursued properly, it can migrate over to the experimenting stage. Within this stage, the parties to the newborn relationship test the waters to see if there is potential for a partnership of some sort in the future. Once past this stage, successful relationships only grow in intensity. Lives become intertwined, and parties to the relationship may experience a deep, soulful bond. This is the pinnacle of any relationship be it familial, romantic or business. However, relationships seldom fixate on this blissful plain of coexistence. Sadly, oneness is only an illusion fostered briefly in the minds of many star-struck lovers, parents of seemingly perfect children or sales managers watching new hire sales numbers hit the roof. Similarly, the bloom may slip easily off the rose when a loving child turns into a fiercely delinquent teenager or a rock star account manager begins to slip in monthly sales. The expectations that one or both parties have for one another are often betrayed by stark reality, and the parties to the relationship may view this divergence from stellar expectations as an unforgiveable transgression. Mature relationships can withstand differentiation, but less robust relationships may slide down a slippery slope into 'circumscribing.' The relationship cramps one's style, and becomes an albatross around one's neck. It is at this point that relationships slide further into perilous stagnation. Without counselling or other relationship management, the relationship becomes a thing to avoid. The beloved boyfriend stops returning calls or the Account Manager is no longer invited on high profile customer engagements. At this juncture, the relationship is one step away from termination or inevitable death.

Impending relationship death needs to be addressed poste-haste, or else one risks being left with only a post-mortem to perform. The relationship will evaporate into an eternity of what-ifs and regrets. A solid knowledge of relationship beginnings, middles and ends can only improve the likelihood that problems can be identified and rectified prior to the complete devastation of the bond. Knowledge of the lifecycle is useful, but may not provide sufficient insight to solve all problems. Further attention to the role various dichotomies play in relationships is needed.[24] Connection versus autonomy speaks to the role that each person's independence plays in pairings. Successful relationships meld a delicate blend of togetherness and separateness, such that each partner may maintain secure attachment without threat of losing one's self. Predictability versus novelty entails that relationships maintain some degree of spontaneity and surprise while still maintaining a stable and secure core. Openness versus privacy honors each partner's need to withhold self-disclosure while still maintaining a spirit of openness within the pairing. These and similar factors taken with a solid understanding of relationship initiation, building and maintenance ensure that longevity is in the relationship's future.

Conclusion

The social milieu is here to stay. Participants in today's society will need to learn and master more ways to interact than ever before. Failure to do so condemns one to irrelevance. Online networking, blogging and general maintenance of an Internet presence only add to the pressure of professional glad-handing, dating, and other forms of traditional interacting. These are daunting responsibilities for anyone. However, persons suffering from social anxiety issues are severely impacted. Fortunately, as case studies show, there are a wide variety of resources available to persons experiencing anxiety. Case studies such as those of Abraham Lincoln and Warren Buffett tout amazing success stories. Further, the mysteries of seemingly abstract and ineffable qualities such as 'likeability' are now laid bare. 'Personal Success' authors and theorists like Napoleon Hill lay the ground work for studies on personal qualities that invite others to like one. Hill's oeuvre has since been expanded upon and countless others have contributed to the swelling volume of books and other literature that teach people the bare essentials to promote one's own amiability. Sufferers of anxiety—and others interested in the topic—need not spend their time in libraries, nor do they need to expend countless hours researching the topic. The same Internet that forces sociability also provides key resources that help persons cultivate it. Clear and concise lists exist that are packed with relevant information on the subject. Persons can find short, simple, step-by-step troubleshooting tips for virtually any relationship problem. Persons can pull up conversation troubleshooting tips, relationship strategies, social anxiety quick fixes, and just about anything else with only a few key strokes. These resources have proved valuable to many, and persons with any concern pertaining to social interaction would be wise to investigate them.

Social interaction is the key to life's success. People are social animals and cannot thrive in a vacuum. Interaction of all kinds is essential to establish a sense of belonging. Social interaction is needed to validate their experiences, and—when favorable—it provides the self with a deep sense of recognition, acknowledgement and endorsement. For these very reasons, it is especially needed when people are in distress. Thus, this book serves as a reminder that positive social interaction and resultant personal success is within the means of anyone.

Final Word/About the Author

I was born and raised in Norwalk, Connecticut. Growing up, I could often be found spending afternoons reading in the local public library about management techniques and leadership styles, along with overall outlooks towards life. It was from spending those afternoons reading about how others have led productive lives that I was inspired to start studying patterns of human behavior and self-improvement. Usually I write works around sports to learn more about influential athletes in the hopes that from my writing, you the reader can walk away inspired to put in an equal if not greater amount of hard work and perseverance to pursue your goals. If there were one key takeaway from this book it would be that you don't need to be the most outgoing person in the world to develop and cultivate lasting and meaningful relationships in your life. All it takes is a conscious decision to be open to introducing yourself to new people. If you enjoyed *How to be Likeable: The Ultimate Guide to Connecting, Relating, and Creating Authentic Lasting Relationships with People* please leave a review! Also, you can read more of my works on *Bargain Shopping, Productivity Hacks, Morning Meditation, Becoming a Father,* and *LinkedIn: Life Lessons Learned from the "If I Were 22" Campaign* in the Kindle Store.

Endnotes

[1] "Online Etymology Dictionary." *Online Etymology Dictionary.* N.p., n.d. Web.

[2] Allan, Kenneth D. "Beginning to See: A Sociological Core." *Explorations in Classical Sociological Theory: Seeing the Social World.* Los Angeles: SAGE, 2013. 12. Print.

[3] Molleman, Lucas, Ido Pen, and Franz J. Weissing. "Effects of Conformism on the Cultural Evolution of Social Behaviour." *PLOS ONE.* N.p., 10 July 2013. Web.

[4] Waytz, Adam. "Humans Are By Nature Social Animals." Edge. Edge Foundation, 2014. Web.

[5] Markham, Art, Ph.D. "Why Other People Are the Key to Our Happiness." *Ulterior Motives.* N.p., 22 July 2014. Web.

[6] Harmon, Katherine. "Social Ties Boost Survival by 50 Percent." *Scientific American Global RSS.* N.p., 28 July 2010. Web.

[7] USA. Stanislaus County. Stanislaus County of Education. By Tom Changnon. N.p.: n.p., n.d. *Importance of Social Interactions.* Web.

[8] Freeborn, Donna, Ph.D. "Older Adults and the Importance of Social Interaction." *Online Medical Encyclopedia*. University of Rochester Medical Center, n.d. Web.

[9] Simpson, Brent. "Altruism and Indirect Reciprocity: The Interaction of Person and Situation in Prosocial Behavior." *Social Psychology Quarterly* 71.1 (2008): 37-52. Greater Good. University of California Berkeley. Web.

[10] Richards, Thomas A., Ph.D. "What Is Social Anxiety?" *Social Anxiety Institute*. N.p., n.d. Web.

[11] Mayo Clinic Staff. "Social Anxiety Disorder (social Phobia)." *Mayo Clinic*. N.p., n.d. Web.

[12] Hickey, Joseph V. "Chapter 5." *Society in Focus: An Introduction to Sociology*. By William E. Thompson. 5th ed. Boston: Allyn & Bacon, 2005. 128-30. Print.

[13] Borreli, Lizette. "5 Habits Of Very Likeable People." *Medical Daily*. N.p., 22 May 2014. Web.

[14] Siegel, Robert. "Exploring Abraham Lincoln's 'Melancholy.'" *NPR*. NPR, 26 Oct. 2005. Web.

[15] Leidner, Gordon. "Lincoln the Transformational Leader." *Great American History*. N.p., 26 Oct. 2005. Web.

[16] Lubin, Julie Zeveloff and Gus. "15 Frugal Billionaires Who Live Like Regular People." *Business Insider*. Business Insider, Inc, 16 Jan. 2013. Web.

[17] Gallo, Camino. "How Warren Buffett And Joel Osteen Conquered Their Terrifying Fear Of Public Speaking." *Forbes*. Forbes Magazine, 16 May 2013. Web.

[18] Madigan, Catherine. "Billionaire Overcomes Fear of Public Speaking." *Shyness & Social Anxiety Treatment Australia*. N.p., 23 Apr. 2013. Web.

[19] Rubin, Ron, and Stuart A. Gold. "The Power of 'Acting As If'" *BeliefNet*. N.p., Apr. 2014. Web.

[20] "Napoleon Hill." *Wikipedia*. Wikimedia Foundation, 12 Jan. 2014. Web.

[21] Feloni, Richard. "14 Habits of Exceptionally Likeable People." *Business Insider*. N.p., 22 May 2014. Web.

[22] "The Secret: Whatever Your Mind Can Conceive And Believe, It Can Achieve." *The Mind Unleashed*. N.p., 7 Dec. 2013. Web.

[23] Konrath, Jill. "3 Sales Follow-Up Strategies to Replace

'Touching Base.'" Weblog post. *Jillkonrath*. N.p., n.d.

[24] "Interpersonal Relationships." *Psychology20*. Wikispaces, n.d. Web.